SHW

THEMATIC UNIT

Presidents' Day and Martin Luther King, Jr. Day

Written by Mary Ellen Sterling

Illustrated by Keith Vasconcelles

Teacher Created Materials, Inc.
6421 Industry Way
Westminster, CA 92683
www.teachercreated.com
©1992 Teacher Created Materials, Inc.
Reprinted, 2002
Made in U.S.A.
ISBN 1-55734-262-8

Table of Contents

Introduction

Presidents' Day and Martin Luther King, Jr. Day contains a captivating, whole language, thematic unit about celebrating and honoring three great leaders. Its 80 exciting reproducible pages are filled with a variety of lesson ideas designed for use with primary children.

At its core are three books—*My First Martin Luther King Book, A Picture Book of Abraham Lincoln,* and *A Picture Book of George Washington.* For each of these selections, activities are included which set the stage for reading, encourage the enjoyment of the book, and extend the concepts gained. In addition, the theme is connected to the curriculum with activities in language arts (including daily writing suggestions), math, science, social studies, art, music, and life skills (cooking, physical education, etc.). Many of these activities encourage cooperative learning. Suggestions and patterns for bulletin boards and unit management tools are additional time savers for the busy teacher. Furthermore, directions for student-created Big Books and a culminating activity, which allows students to synthesize their knowledge in order to produce products that can be shared beyond the classroom, highlight this very complete teacher resource.

This thematic unit includes:

❏ **literature selections**—summaries of stories with related lessons (complete with reproducible pages) that cross the curriculum.

❏ **poetry**—suggested selections and lessons enabling students to write and publish their own works.

❏ **planning guides**—suggestions for sequencing lessons each day of the unit.

❏ **writing ideas**—daily suggestions as well as writing activities across the curriculum, including Big Books.

❏ **bulletin board ideas**—suggestions and plans for student-created and/or interactive bulletin boards.

❏ **homework suggestions**—extending the unit to the child's home.

❏ **curriculum connections**—in language arts, math, science, social studies, art, music, and life skills.

❏ **group projects**—to foster cooperative learning.

❏ **a culminating activity**—which requires students to synthesize their learning to produce a product or engage in an activity that can be shared with others.

❏ **a bibliography**—suggesting additional literature and non-fiction books on the theme.

To keep this valuable resource intact so that it can be used year after year, you may wish to punch holes in the pages and store them in a three-ring binder.

Introduction *(cont.)*

Why Whole Language?

A whole language approach involves children in using all modes of communication: reading, writing, listening, observing, illustrating, experiencing, and doing. Communication skills are interconnected and integrated into lessons that emphasize the whole of language rather than isolating its parts. The lessons revolve around selected literature. Reading is not taught as a separate subject from writing and spelling, for example. A child reads, writes (spelling appropriately for his/her level), speaks, listens, etc. in response to a literature experience introduced by the teacher. In this way, language skills grow naturally, stimulated by involvement and interest in the topic at hand.

Why Thematic Planning?

One very useful tool for implementing an integrated whole language program is thematic planning. By choosing a theme with correlating literature selections for a unit of study, a teacher can plan activities throughout the day that lead to a cohesive, in-depth study of the topic. Students will be practicing and applying their skills in meaningful context. Consequently, they will tend to learn and retain more. Both teachers and students will be freed from a day that is broken into unrelated segments of isolated drill and practice.

Why Cooperative Learning?

Besides academic skills and content, students need to learn social skills. No longer can this area of development be taken for granted. Students must learn to work cooperatively in groups in order to function well in modern society. Group activities should be a regular part of school life, and teachers should consciously include social objectives as well as academic objectives in the planning. For example, a group working together to write a report may need to select a leader. The teacher should make the objectives clear to the students and monitor the qualities of good leader-follower group interaction just as he/she would state and monitor the academic goals of the projects.

Why Big Books?

An excellent, cooperative, whole language activity is the production of Big Books. Groups of students or the whole class can apply their language skills, content knowledge, and creativity to produce a Big Book that can become a part of the classroom to be read and reread. These books make excellent culminating projects for sharing beyond the classroom with parents, librarians, and other classes. Big Books can be produced in many ways. This thematic unit book includes directions for one method you may choose.

Notes About the Holidays

Martin Luther King, Jr. Day

In 1983, the Congress of the United States set aside the third Monday in January as a federal holiday to honor the life of Martin Luther King, Jr. This date falls near his birthday, January 15. It is a day for remembering and rededication to the principles for which he stood—freedom, justice, and equal rights for all, achieved through peaceful means.

Presidents' Day

Presidents' Day is celebrated on the third Monday in February. It is a day to remember all those who have served as presidents of the United States. Lincoln's birthday (February 12) and Washington's birthday (February 22) were traditionally celebrated as separate holidays, and in some states this is still true. Combining them into one day provided a more universal opportunity to recognize their contributions as well as those of all our presidents. School children typically are involved in patriotic studies around this time.

Using this Thematic Unit

The sections on the three great Americans featured in this book may be used in several sequences. Choose the order below which fits the needs of your classroom.

• Birthday Order

Dr. King's birthday is celebrated the third Monday in January. When the actual birthday of Martin Luther King, Jr. (January 15, 1929) draws near, use the section beginning on page 6. Go on to the Lincoln section (pages 19–31) as Lincoln's birthday, February 12, approaches. Follow with the George Washington section (pages 32–44) around his birthday, February 22.

• Two-Holiday Order

Complete the section on Martin Luther King, Jr. in January around the third Monday, Martin Luther King, Jr. Day. Study Washington first and Lincoln second around Presidents' Day, the third Monday in February. This will help reinforce the concept that Washington was our first president and Lincoln came later as our sixteenth president.

• Historical Order

Study Washington first, Lincoln second, and Martin Luther King, Jr. third to provide students with a better perspective of the roles of these three great men in the history of our country. The emphasis of a unit organized in this sequence could be: Three Great Freedom Fighters. Students could focus on the freedom and rights each was seeking and the methods used to achieve their objectives.

My First Martin Luther King Book

by Dee Lillegard

In this book, the life story of Martin Luther King is presented in a unique poetry format. Each poem focuses on a different event in the life of Dr. King and is accompanied by a vivid illustration. The language employed by the author is simple and her messages are allowed to come through clearly. As the students read and learn about Martin Luther King's life, they will see that in many ways he was just like them. He was also an extraordinary man with a vision and a plan that lives on today.

The outline below is a suggested plan for using the various activities that are presented in this unit. You may adapt these ideas to fit your own classroom situation.

Sample Plan

Lesson I

- Background Information: Learn about Georgia (page 10)

- Brainstorm the meaning of prejudice (#2, top of page 7).

- Have students write what they know about Dr. King (#3, top of page 7).

- Read My *First Martin Luther King Book.*

Lesson II

- Begin Page by Page activities. Choose one or more of the activities to complete (page 11).

- Tell about your dream for peace. Draw a picture (see page 12).

- Write initial poems (see page 13).

- Learn more about the life and work of Martin Luther King, Jr. (see page 17).

Lesson III

- Continue Page by Page activities (page 11).

- Describe colors (page 13).

- Critical Thinking Character traits on page 15

- Art: Commemorative plate (page 17)

Lesson IV

- Continue Page by Page activities (page 11).

- Lists of favorite words (page 13)

- Skip-counting activity (page 16)

- Inferences. Identifying facts and non-facts (page 15)

Lesson V

- Role play story events (page 17).

- Read other books with the theme of prejudice (#4, page 8).

- Big Book Idea (#5, page 8)

Overview of Activities

SETTING THE STAGE

1. Learn the words and music of the Civil Rights song, "We Shall Overcome." One source for the words and music is *If You Lived at the Time of Martin Luther King* by Ellen Levine (Scholastic, 1990). It can also be found, along with the text of the "I Have a Dream" speech, in the appendices of *Martin Luther King: The Peaceful Warrior* by Ed Clayton (Simon & Schuster, 1968). Listen to a recording of the song, if possible. Discuss the meaning of the lyrics.

2. With the students, brainstorm the meaning of prejudice. Talk about instances in which they have experienced prejudice because of age, race, or sex.

3. Tell students that they will be learning about Dr. Martin Luther King, Jr. Ask them what they know about this famous leader. Have them record their responses (see sample worksheet on page 9). Save the papers for later use. At the end of the unit, return the papers and let students write what they have learned.

4. Dr. King was born in Atlanta, Georgia. The area around his birthplace, church, and tomb is called The Martin Luther King, Jr. National Historic Site. Learn about Martin Luther King's home state of Georgia. Have the students complete the activity sheet on page 10. You may want the children to write some more Georgia facts on the back of that page.

5. Begin reading aloud *My First Martin Luther King Book.* Some suggested ways to present the pages of his text are outlined at the bottom of Page by Page (page 11).

ENJOYING THE BOOK

1. Continue to use the suggested activities from page 11 as the different poems are read. Students may be paired or grouped to work together on some projects. You may want them to work individually on other activities.

2. Creative Writing. On page 13, there are five different activities from which to choose. Students can write poems, descriptive phrases, or new verses for "We Shall Overcome." They may also write about their favorite words or construct a chart of soul foods and non-soul foods. Choose those projects best suited for the skill levels of your students.

Soul Food	Not Soul Food

3. Continue to learn about Martin Luther King. Have the students fill in the blanks and the word puzzle on page 14.

Overview of Activities *(cont.)*

ENJOYING THE BOOK *(cont.)*

4. Develop critical thinking skills. Two possible methods are outlined on page 15. In the first activity, students are asked to identify characteristics of Martin Luther King. Then they must cite evidence(s) of this characteristic through specific examples within the text. Students may be asked to complete a sentence frame (see below) for this activity.

> *Martin Luther King was* _____
>
> *I know this because* _____

5. Help students learn to locate supporting material for factual statements. Note that there may be disagreements about what is inferred. It is the process which is most important, rather than having the right or wrong answer. (See page 15.)

EXTENDING THE BOOK

1. Sample some fresh peaches. Ask the produce person at the supermarket if they are Georgia peaches. Prepare peach pie or peach cobbler as a class project, or serve peaches with ice cream.

2. Learn about the peaceful protest of 1963 in which a quarter of a million people marched on Washington, D.C. to demand equal rights for blacks. Students can use their skip-counting skills to help figure out the name of this historic event. (See A Peaceful Protest, page 16.)

3. To Discuss and Do, the nine activities on page 17 are suggested follow-ups to your studies about Martin Luther King. You may want to read correlating stories to the class, stage a boycott, role play, or make a commemorative plate. Choose those activities that are best-suited to your teaching style and the skill level of the students.

4. Read other books about prejudice. Appropriate titles include *But Names Will Never Hurt Me* by Bernard Waber (Houghton Mifflin, 1976); *Crow Boy* by Taro Yashima (Viking Press, 1955); *Tico and the Golden Wings* by Leo Lionni (Peter Smith, 1993).

5. Big Book Idea. Trace around each student's body onto butcher paper. Direct the children to cut out the forms and draw their own portraits, clothes, and other features. Tell them to write their dreams for peace on the body. Join all the paper bodies by the hand and line the classroom walls with them.

Martin Luther King Facts

1. Write or draw some things you know about Martin Luther King, Jr.

2. Write or draw some things you have learned about Martin Luther King, Jr.

Georgia

Martin Luther King, Jr. grew up in Atlanta, Georgia. Find out about Martin's home state. Read and follow the directions below.

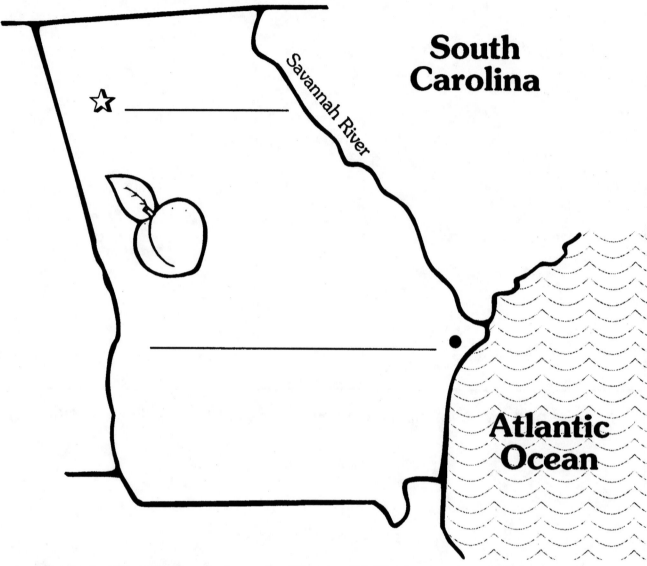

1. Martin Luther King was born in Atlanta. Write the name, Atlanta, on the space next to the (☆).

2. Georgia is famous for its peaches. It is called the Peach State. Color the (🍑) orange.

3. Savannah is a seaport city in Georgia. Write the name Savannah on the space next to the (●)

4. Part of Georgia's eastern border is the Savannah River. Color the river blue.

5. The (〰〰) show the Atlantic Ocean. Color the ocean blue-green.

Page by Page

After a first reading of *My First Martin Luther King Book,* the pages may be reviewed in any number of ways (page-by-page, two at a time, etc.). Whichever way you choose, follow up the pages with any or all of the following activities.

Three Boys: Tell or write how you would feel if you were not allowed to play with a friend who was a different color.

M.L.: Write your initials. Write some other names using the same initials.

Shoes: Fold a sheet of paper in fourths. In each section, write something about yourself of which you're proud. Draw pictures.

Bicycle: Tell about a new toy you would like to have. Write some ways you could earn money to buy that toy.

Words: Get a dictionary. Copy six big words.

Books: Go to the library. Copy the titles of some books that you have really enjoyed reading or that you would like to read.

A Voice: Learn the words and music to "We Shall Overcome" (see page 72 of *If You Lived at the Time of Martin Luther King* by Ellen Levine, Scholastic, 1990).

Football: Explain how to play football. Or choose another team sport and tell why all players must work together as a team.

Coretta: Both Martin and Coretta were leaders. Write about some qualities that you think make a person a good leader.

A Leader: What is the Nobel Peace Prize? Research and find out why Martin Luther King, Jr. received this award.

A Dream: Martin dreamed about freedom for all. Write about your dreams; draw a picture (use page 12 if desired).

Bus Ride: Draw a picture of a bus. Show boys and girls of all colors riding on the bus. Study the Montgomery Bus Boycott. See the second activity on page 17 for a suggested source.

Color: Draw a picture of yourself. Give yourself a coat of many colors.

Freedom: Finish this sentence: Freedom is….

Extensions:

- Read the poem "Martin Luther King Day" (from *Celebrations* by Myra Cohn Livingston, Holiday House, 1985).

- Have the children write their own poems about Martin Luther King, Jr.

- Pair or group the children. Assign each pair or group a different page from *My First Martin Luther King Book*. Direct them to draw a picture to illustrate that poem.

- Read and learn about the holiday for Dr. King. A good source is *Martin Luther King Day* by Linda Lowery (Lerner, 1987).

Name_____

I Have a Dream

Martin Luther King had a dream that some day all people of all colors would be able to live together in peace. Tell about your dream for peace. Draw a picture to go with your story.

Creative Writing Ideas

On this page you will find a number of easy methods for motivating creative writing. Assign a different one each day; give students a choice between two ideas or use one for a homework activity.

Initial Poems

Establish that Martin's nickname was M.L.—the letters stood for Martin Luther. Ask students to describe Martin using words that begin with the letters of his initials. One possible example is Mighty Leader—Kind man. After they have written some M.L.K. poems, direct them to write poems about themselves using their own initials.

Colors

Reread "Color" from *My First Martin Luther King Book*. Have the children choose a color. Tell them to write descriptions of that color. Encourage the use of adjectives and descriptive phrases.

Blue is the sparkling water in my plastic swimming pool.

We Shall Overcome

Group the students. Direct them to write the words for a new verse of "We Shall Overcome." Have them sing their verses for the whole class.

Favorite Words

Have the students make personal lists of their favorite words. Then direct them to copy the following unfinished sentence, writing it separately for each favorite word: One of my favorite words is

_____ because _____.

> *One of my favorite words is*
> *serendipity because it makes me*
> *giggle when I hear it.*

Soul Food

Martin Luther King liked to eat soul food such as pork and black-eyed peas. Have the students write their own recipes for preparing black-eyed peas or another soul food. Extend the activity with a chart of soul foods and non-soul foods. Draw illustrations or cut out pictures from magazines to add to the chart.

Martin Luther King, Jr. Puzzle

Learn about Martin Luther King, Jr. Read each sentence below. Fill in the blanks; use the Word Bank. Write the words in the puzzle. Use the word that goes down below the arrow to fill in the blank in the sentence below the puzzle.

1. As a child he sang in a ___ ___ u ___ ___ ___ choir.

2. Martin Luther King Jr. was a ___ ___ ___ ___ ___ f ___ ___ leader.

3. He became ___ ___ ___ t ___ ___ of a church in Alabama.

4. Dr. King led ___ a ___ ___ ___ ___ ___ for peace.

5. Dr. King said, "I have a d ___ ___ ___ ___ ."

6. He asked people to work for ___ q ___ ___ ___ rights.

7. Dr. King was awarded the ___ ___ ___ e ___ Peace Prize.

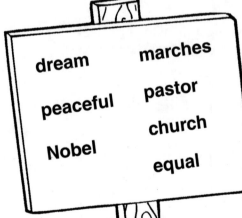

Word Bank

dream   marches

peaceful   pastor

church

Nobel   equal

2. _ _ _ _ _ ☐ _ _
1. _ _ _ ☐ _ _ _
6. _ _ ☐ _ _ _
7. _ _ _ ☐ _
5. _ ☐ _ _ _
2. _ _ _ _ _ ☐ _ _
4. _ ☐ _ _ _ _ _

Martin Luther King, Jr. dreamed of _____ for all people.

Critical Thinking Skills

Two different methods to develop critical thinking skills are described below. Incorporate them into your lesson plans wherever they best fit.

Character Traits1

Model with the students the following process. Identify a character trait of Martin Luther King. For example, he was persistent. Ask the students to find evidence of this fact within the text of *My First Martin Luther King Book.* In this case, when he played football and fell, he got up again (page 19). Have the students copy the sentence frame in the box below. As a class, brainstorm some of Martin Luther King's character traits and record them on the chalkboard, chart paper, or overhead projector. Direct the students to complete the sentence frame.

Martin Luther King was _____

I know this because _____

Some possible traits include: responsible, proud, fair, strong, studious, a peaceful leader, a dreamer.

Supporting Statements

Sometimes the answer to a question can be found directly on a page of text. Others have to be inferred or "figured out" using supporting statements. If, for example, you were to state that Martin Luther King was a reader, you could support this fact with the information on page 15. "He loved reading.... He read a whole mountain of books."

Another statement about King might say that he liked to eat yogurt. No information in this book is provided to support this. With the students, determine which of the following can be supported by the text in *My First Martin Luther King Book.*

1. Martin Luther King was famous.

2. He was a hard worker.

3. Martin liked to read about George Washington.

4. He was proud that he was black.

5. Everyone liked Martin Luther King's ideas.

A Peaceful Protest

On August 28, 1963, 250,000 people of all races went to Washington, D.C. to march for equal rights for Black-Americans. They wanted the government to do something about unfair practices.

At this gathering, Dr. King made his famous "I Have a Dream" speech. In the speech, he told of his dream that someday children of all colors could come together and play.

Find out the name of this peaceful protest. Count by twos. Circle the letters and write them on the lines below.

G	(M)	S	(A)	U	R	V	C	T
1	2	3	4	5	6	7	8	9
H	L	O	B	N	K	W	N	A
10	11	12	13	14	15	16	17	18
F	S	R	H	Q	I	T	N	J
19	20	21	22	23	24	25	26	27
G	D	T	I	O	E	N	We shall overcome!
28	29	30	31	32	33	34	

M   A   ___   ___   ___   ___   ___
2   4   6   8   10   12   14

___   ___   ___   ___   ___   ___   ___   ___   ___   ___
16   18   20   22   24   26   28   30   32   34

To Discuss and Do

The activities on this page may be incorporated into your studies while you are extending the *My First Martin Luther King Book.* Choose those ideas and projects which are most compatible with your teaching style and needs.

* Ask the students to define prejudice and explain what it means to them. Talk about some reasons people might be prejudiced (fear, ignorance, echoing, parents' statements, etc.). Discuss ways that people could overcome their prejudice (take time to learn about others, discussions about fears, cooperate with others, etc.).

* Read aloud to the students a story about Rosa Parks and the ensuing bus boycott (*Rosa Parks and the Montgomery Bus Boycott* by Teresa Celsi, Millbrook Press, 1991). How many students think they could be as brave as Ms. Parks?

* Define boycott. Stage a pretend (or real) boycott of an unjust situation at school or within the community. Make signs and banners; plan a march.

* Role play the "Shoes" incident (page 9) or the "Three Boys" (page 5). Ask students how it felt to be told where to sit in a store or that they could not play with a friend.

* Sample some soul foods. If possible, prepare a dish in class. Invite adult volunteers to prepare and explain the food preparation to the class.

* Read aloud to the students "The Silent Lobby" from *The Big Book of Peace,* ed. by Ann Durell and Marilyn Sachs (Dutton Children's Books, 1990). Discuss the present status of voting rights. Are these rights still being denied to some?

* Make a commemorative plate of Dr. Martin Luther King. Give each child a paper plate and some crayons. Tell them to draw a picture of Dr. King on the plate. Students may also write stories or words or cut out pictures to decorate the plate. Take a 5" x 8" (12.5 cm x 20 cm) index card and fold the bottom 2" (5 cm) upward (1). Turn the card over and fold the top evenly in half toward the bottom (2). Place the plate in the upward fold (3).

* Find Georgia on a map of the United States. Name the states that border Georgia. Draw an outline of the state and write some facts about Georgia in the outline.

* Martin Luther King Day is celebrated in January. Many cities have named streets or buildings after him. Find out what your community has done or is planning to do to honor him.

Martin Luther King, Jr. Words

speeches	Atlanta, Georgia	rights
January 15	"White Only"	shot
minister	Montgomery, Alabama	violence
Coretta Scott	marches	protests
freedom	prejudice	doctorate
boycott	leader	buses
bus	sang	riots
Rosa Parks	choir	equality
March on Washington	James Earl Ray	pride
I Have a Dream . . .	3rd Monday in January	liberty

This Word Bank is a handy reference tool for creative writing, vocabulary development, social studies, and more. It can also be used with the story frame on page 45.

We shall overcome.

A Picture Book of Abraham Lincoln
by David A. Adler

Summary

This colorfully illustrated biography is a good source of information on Abraham Lincoln for primary children. Starting with his birth and ending with his death, the book relates main events in Abraham Lincoln's life. Frequent glimpses at Lincoln's personality and character are provided to the reader as well. Important dates in Abraham Lincoln's life are listed at the end of the book.

The outline below is a suggested plan for using the various activities that are presented in this unit. You may adapt these ideas to fit your own classroom situation.

Sample Plan

Lesson I

- Brainstorm what children know about Lincoln; save for future use (page 20)

- Vocabulary: Preview words from the story. Select from Lincoln Word Bank (page 31)

- Read *A Picture Book of Abraham Lincoln*.

Lesson II

- Recall some story details; do a critical thinking exercise (page 22)

- Language: Write a letter to Lincoln.

- Art: Draw a Lincoln penny (page 20)

- Knowledge: To Talk About (page 24)

- Word Game (page 25)

Lesson III

- Phonics: Hidden messages—Inside Lincoln's Stovepipe (page 27)

- Social Studies: Who's the President? (page 28)

- Math: Abe Lincoln's Groceries (page 26)

- Continue with To Talk About (page 24)

Lesson IV

- Math/Geography: Lincoln's Homes (page 30)

- Writing: Cut and assemble your own book (page 29)

- Research: Students read other books about Lincoln and share what they have learned.

- Continue with To Talk About (page 24)

Lesson V

- Big Book: Write a book about Lincoln (page 22)

- Sing freedom songs (page 64)

- Learn about the author. Read other books by David Adler (page 47)

- Make a patriotic dessert (page 65)

- Students compare what they have learned about Lincoln to what they already knew (see Lesson I)

Overview of Activities

SETTING THE STAGE
---

1. Penny Rubbings. Each child will need a penny for this activity (either supply the pennies for the whole class or request that the children each bring one to school). Have the children identify the man pictured on the coin. Establish the fact that Abraham Lincoln was President of the United States many, many years ago. Give each child a plain sheet of paper and a red or blue colored pencil. Direct the children to place their coins face up on their desks. Have them cover the penny with the sheet of paper. Show them how to hold their pencils sideways so they can rub the paper over the surface of the penny. This may take some practice. The children may make as many rubbings as they'd like on the page using both red and blue colored pencils.

2. Extend the penny rubbing activity. Show other coins and bills and identify the famous people on them. Give each child a round paper plate. Tell the children to design their own coins. They can draw a picture of a hero or an important historical figure, or they may choose to draw a self-portrait. Crayons, colored markers, or colored pencils can be used to complete this project.

3. Establish facts about Lincoln. Ask the children what they know about Lincoln. Record appropriate responses on the chalkboard or chart paper and save for future use. (For some quick facts about Lincoln, see page 61.) Follow-up activities: Have the students copy some of these facts on a sheet of paper. Tell the children to write a short story about Lincoln, using the recorded facts.

4. Tell the children that the book you are going to read to them is about Abraham Lincoln's life.

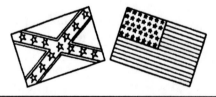

ENJOYING THE BOOK
---

1. Knowledge and Comprehension. Use the questions on page 24 to assess the students' recall of facts and understanding of the text. Discuss a number of questions each day.

2. Reinforce vocabulary words with a game like the one described on page 25. Use the words given or your own choices.

Overview of Activities *(cont.)*

ENJOYING THE BOOK *(cont.)*

3. Art. Build log cabins like Abraham Lincoln did. Follow the directions on page 23.

4. Phonics. Review initial consonant and vowel sounds to discover what is hidden in Lincoln's stovepipe hat. A worksheet is provided on page 27. Extend the activity by having students write a secret message of their own or having them tell some other things that could be hidden inside a stovepipe hat.

5. Language Arts. *A Picture Book of Abraham Lincoln* is a biography. Have the students write their own biographical books. Share that a biography is the story of someone's life. Use the cover on page 28.

6. Art. Students can finish drawing the picture of Lincoln on page 29. Then they may make miniature three-dimensional stovepipe hats. Simply cut a sheet of black construction paper to fit around a cardboard toilet paper tube. Glue the paper to the tube. Cut a black construction paper circle about 1/2-inch (1.25 cm) larger than the circumference of the tube and glue to the bottom of the tube.

For a stovepipe hat that children can wear, cut the center from a paper plate for the brim. Along the long edge of a 12" x 18" (30 cm x 45 cm) piece of construction paper, cut 1" (2.5 cm) slits every 2" (5 cm) or so. Roll the paper into a tube and tape. Slide the tube through the hole in the paper plate and bend up tabs under the brim. Glue, tape, or staple into place.

 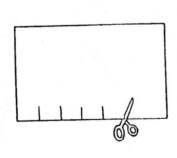 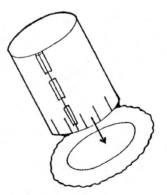 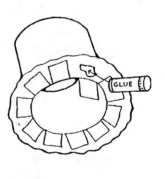

7. Math. Fill a jar with pennies. On a piece of paper, have each child write his/her name and an estimate of how many pennies are contained in the jar. With the class, count the pennies. Give a prize to the closest estimate.

Examine a five dollar bill. Which president is depicted on it? (Lincoln) Create some money word problems for the children to solve or use page 48.

Overview of Activities *(cont.)*

ENYOYING THE BOOK *(cont.)*

8. Critical Thinking. Have the students compare themselves to Abraham Lincoln. What qualities do they share with him? What physical characteristics do they have in common? Students may record their comparisons in paragraph form or in a Venn diagram.

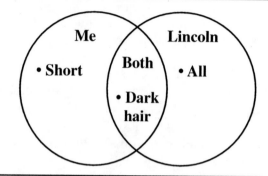

EXTENDING THE BOOK

1. Big Book. Using the information they have learned about Abraham Lincoln, have students create their own Big Book about him to share with younger students. Brainstorm important events that should be included. Assign a different event to each group. Have them write the text and draw an illustration on an 12" x 18" (30 cm x 46 cm) piece of white construction paper. Sequence the pages in the order of events and bind them together with a cover.

2. Learn some freedom songs. The words to four popular songs are on page 64. Accompanying music can be found in *Wee Sing America: Songs of Patriots and Pioneers* by Pamela Conn Beall and Susan Hagen Nipp (Price Stern Sloan, 1987). Listen to recordings of these songs.

3. Make a patriotic dessert. See page 65 for a sampling of easy-to-prepare treats.

4. Compare what students have learned about Lincoln with what they initially knew. Add new facts to the chart begun in #3 of Setting the Stage on page 21. New facts can be written in a different color of chalk or ink, if desired.

5. Learn about the author. Read some other books written by David A. Adler. On page 47 you will find a brief biography you may want to share with the students. Listed on the same page are titles of other books Mr. Adler has written. Have the students give oral book reports. Compare two of the author's books in a Venn diagram or chart.

Build a Log Cabin

Materials:

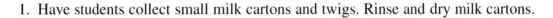

small milk cartons

brown or green construction paper

twigs

glue

tape

Directions:

1. Have students collect small milk cartons and twigs. Rinse and dry milk cartons.

2. Give each student a milk carton.

3. Tape the opening of the milk carton shut.

4. Use glue to attach the twigs to the sides of the milk carton. Do one side at a time, letting each dry before beginning another.

5. After gluing twigs to all four sides, have students cut construction paper to fit like a roof over the top of the milk carton.

6. If brown paper is being used, draw shingles or wood planks on it. If green paper is being used, draw blades of grass on it to make it look like sod.

7. Glue the decorated construction paper to the top of the milk carton to complete the cabin.

To Talk About

Assess students' knowledge and comprehension with the following questions. Suggested answers are provided for you in the parentheses following each question.

1. Where was Abraham Lincoln born? (Kentucky)

2. Did Abraham Lincoln have any brothers or sisters? (an older sister, Sarah, a third child, Thomas, died in infancy.)

3. Where did Abraham Lincoln's family move when he was seven? (Indiana)

4. How did Abraham Lincoln help his father? (chopped down trees, built a fence, cleared land for the farm, built a new log cabin, plowed the fields)

5. What happened to Abraham Lincoln's mother? (died)

6. Did Abraham Lincoln like Sarah Bush Johnston, his stepmother? (yes, called her his angel mother)

7. What did Abraham Lincoln love to do? (read)

8. In 1830, when Abraham Lincoln was 21, his family moved again. To where did they move? (Illinois)

9. What did Abraham Lincoln look like? (tall, thin)

10. Which river did Abraham Lincoln float down on a flatboat built by him and two other men? (Mississippi River)

11. What did Abraham Lincoln see for the first time in New Orleans? (a slave market)

12. How did Abraham Lincoln feel about slavery? (made him miserable, thought it was wrong)

13. When Abraham Lincoln returned to Illinois, where did he work? (in a general store)

14. What was Abraham Lincoln like? (told jokes and stories, he talked about politics, people liked him)

15. After working in the general store what did he do? (he became a lawyer and ran for public office)

16. What happened after Mr. Lincoln became president in 1861? (Eleven southern states withdrew from the United States and formed the Confederate States of America.)

17. On April 12, 1861, Confederate soldiers fired on Fort Sumter, setting into motion what event? (the Civil War)

18. What did the Emancipation Proclamation say? (All slaves were free.)

19. Where did Abraham Lincoln make his famous speech? (Gettysburg, Pennsylvania)

20. The Civil War ended on April 9, 1865. How long had it lasted? (four years)

21. Who won the Civil War? (the North)

22. What did John Wilkes Booth do to Abraham Lincoln on April 14, 1865? (He shot and killed him.)

Word Game

Directions:

Choose a number of words that you would like to reinforce. Make a set of flash cards of these words for each child. Read a sentence aloud to the class. Have the children hold up the word that fits in the blank. Walk around to check the answers. Continue in the same manner until all the sentences have been reviewed. Sample words and sentences can be found below. Add to the list and create your own sentenĪces to fit the words.

Extensions:

- Direct the children to say or write sentences using a particular word.

- Have the children arrange the flash cards in alphabetical order.

- Write the incomplete sentences on the chalkboard. Tell the children to copy each sentence and supply the missing words.

- Pair the children. Tell them to find the words on the cards in the story text. Have them practice reading the sentences to one another.

Read these sentences aloud to the class.

1. Abraham loved to _____ books. *(read)*

2. In 1860 Abraham Lincoln became the sixteenth _____ of the United States of America. *(president)*

3. Abraham Lincoln studied for two years so that he could become a _____. *(lawyer)*

4. One of Abraham Lincoln's nicknames was "_____ Abe." *(Honest)*

5. President Lincoln grew a _____. *(beard)*

6. Mr. Lincoln did not like how _____ were treated. *(slaves)*

7. Abraham called his _____ "angel mother" because he liked her. *(stepmother)*

8. Abraham Lincoln was killed a few days after the _____ ended. *(Civil War)*

Flash Cards. Make a copy for each child. Cut apart on the lines and glue onto index cards.

president	**lawyer**
stepmother	**Honest**
read	**beard**
slaves	**Civil War**

Abe Lincoln's Groceries

When Abraham Lincoln was a young man, he worked in a store in New Salem, Illinois. Use the prices in the box below to figure out the price at which he would have sold these groceries. One has been done for you.

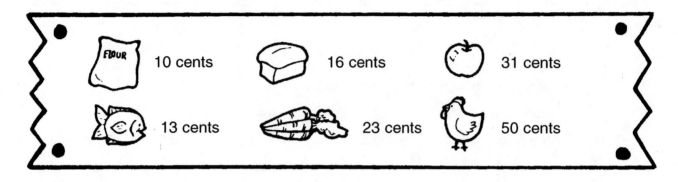

Example:

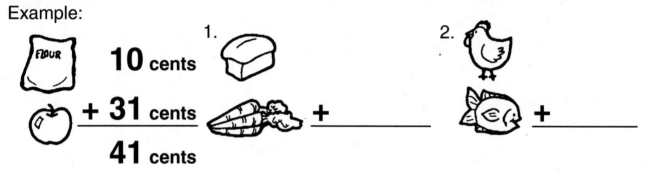

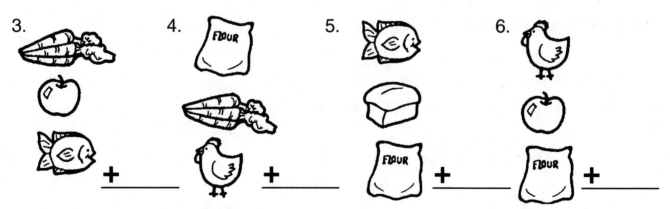

Challenge: How much would…

☆☆ 3 chickens cost? _____

☆☆ 5 sacks of flour cost? _____

☆☆☆ a "fish sandwich" cost? _____

Inside Lincoln's Stovepipe

1. Find out what Abraham Lincoln hid in his stovepipe hat. Write the first letter of each picture on the line below it.

___ ___ ___ ___ ___ ___

___ ___ ___ ___ ___ ___ ___ ___

2. Use pictures to write a secret message to put in your stovepipe hat.

3. Name or draw three other things you could hide in a stovepipe hat.

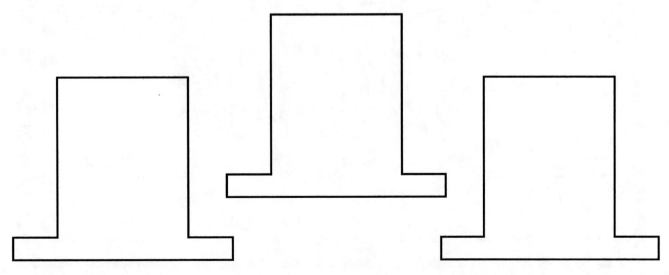

Who's the President?

In 1858, Abraham Lincoln ran for the United States Senate. He lost the election. In 1860, Abraham Lincoln ran for president of the United States and won.

Do you know who the current president and vice president of the United States are?

With some help, find out the answers to the questions below.

1. Who is the president of the United States?

   _____

2. Who is the vice-president of the United States?

   _____

3. How many U.S. senators are there from each state? _____

4. Who are the U.S. senators from your state?

   _____

5. How many U.S. representatives are there from your state? _____

6. Who is the U.S. representative from your district? _____

Your Own Book

Reproduce the page below. Let children make their own pictures on the cover. On the other page let them write and illustrate something from *A Picture Book of Abraham Lincoln.*

A class book can be made by compiling pages that various students have completed.

My Picture Book
of
Abraham Lincoln
Written and Illustrated by

_____

Lincoln's Homes

Abraham Lincoln was born in Kentucky. When he was seven years old, his family moved to Indiana. Fourteen years later they moved to Illinois.

1. Write the answer for each problem in the circle provided.

2. Connect the numbers in the circles in 1-2-3 order to trace Lincoln's route from home to home.

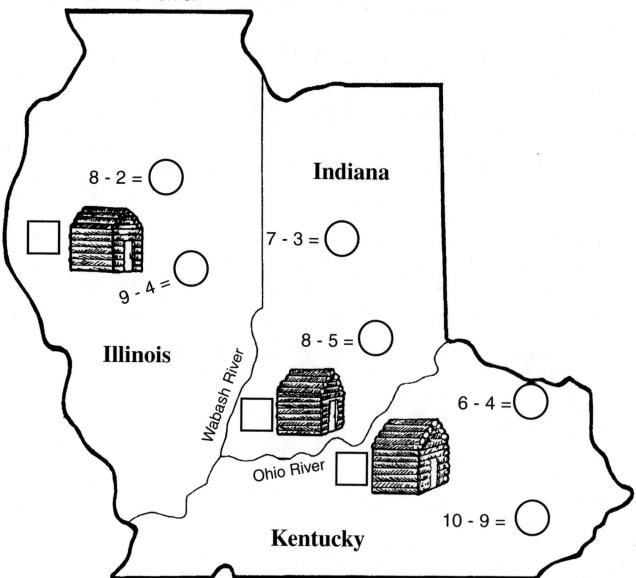

- Write a 1 in the square next to Lincoln's first home.

- Write a 2 in the square next to Lincoln's second home.

- Write a 3 in the square next to Lincoln's third home.

Lincoln Word Bank

This word bank is a handy reference tool for creative writing, vocabulary development, social studies and more. It can also be used with the story frame on page 45.

Abraham Lincoln	theater
February 12	John Wilkes Booth
Kentucky	April 14
books	Confederate
read	Union
Illinois	debates
thin	Mary Todd
beard	public office
general store	stories
laughed	clerk
law	told jokes
lawyer	tall
senate	plowed fields
slavery	Indiana
Civil War	log cabin
Gettysburg Address	"Honest Abe"

stovepipe   frock coat   secret messages   16th president

A *Picture Book of George Washington*

by David A. Adler

Summary

A Picture Book of George Washington *is filled with colorful details and images that evoke the times in which George Washington lived. This book is more than a compilation of pictures, however. It is a fine resource filled with facts about Washington's life. All the basic information that children of this level will need to know is contained within the pages of this resource. On the last page, you will find a listing of important dates in the life of George Washington. After reading this biography, children will have learned a great deal about the "Father of Our Country."*

The outline below is a suggested plan for using the various activities that are presented in this unit. You may adapt these ideas to fit your own classroom situation.

Sample Plan

Lesson I

• Set the stage: Make colonial hats (see page 33)

• Sample fresh cherries; listen to tall tale (#2, top of page 33)

• Chart of George Washington facts (#3, top of page 33)

• Read *A Picture Book of George Washington*

Lesson II

• Read and illustrate the sentences on page 35

• Copy a list of classroom rules (see page 36)

• Math. Number names puzzle on page 37

• Geography. A "Washington" Map (page 38)

Lesson III

• Write about your favorite hobby (page 36)

• Math. One-to-one correspondence (page 39)

• Draw a map of route to school (page 41)

• Read a tall tale (page 41)

Lesson IV

• Compare yourself with George Washington (page 36)

• Fill in the numbers on a calendar (page 40)

• Go for a one-mile walk (page 41)

• Learn about the first flag (page 42)

Lesson V

• Make a Big Book of George Washington's life

• Review how to care for the flag (page 43)

• Make stylized flags (#2, page 34)

Overview of Activities

SETTING THE STAGE

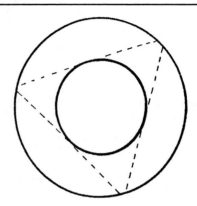

1. Begin this unit by making colonial hats. You will need a large paper grocery bag for each child. Open the bag and flatten it. Cut a circle 12 inches (30 cm) in diameter. Cut out an inside circle about 6 inches (15 cm) in diameter to fit the head. Make three upward folds as indicated by the dashed lines on the pattern at the right. Have the students draw cherry designs on their hats.

2. The children may wear their hats as they sample fresh cherries. Tell the students the tale about George Washington and the cherry tree. According to the legend, when George Washington was a little boy, he chopped down a cherry tree. Upon discovering the damaged tree, George's father asked his young son who had chopped it down. Young George is supposed to have answered that he had done it telling his dad "Father, I cannot tell a lie." Explain that it is probably not factual (a legend) but they are going to learn some true facts about George Washington.

3. Get a feel for colonial times. Show the students pictures of traditional garb of that era. Talk about other famous people of the times, types of transportation, and conveniences that were available then. (You may want to examine the Fact File on page 61.)

4. Begin a chart of George Washington Facts. Add to it throughout the unit.

5. Read *A Picture Book of George Washington.*

ENJOYING THE BOOK

1. Reading Comprehension. Have students illustrate the sentences on page 35. You may wish to use them to create a class Big Book.

2. Creative Writing. The projects on page 36 will give students the opportunity to recall, analyze, and synthesize what they have learned about George Washington. You may want to assign an activity for a meaningful homework experience.

3. Number Names. Expand reading and math skills with Number Words Puzzle on page 37. Challenge the students to find other examples of number names in the text. Extend page 37 by having the students tell or write the events in correct story order.

4. Find Virginia on a map. Locate Mount Vernon and Washington, D.C. Follow up with a mapping exercise (see page 38).

Overview of Activities *(cont.)*

ENJOYING THE BOOK *(cont.)*

5. Fun with Math. A number of hands-on math activities are outlined on page 39. Incorporate them into your curriculum where you feel they are most appropriate. Changes may have to be made depending on the skill and ability levels of the class.

6. This and That (page 41) is a compilation of geography, social studies, math, and writing ideas for use with this unit. You may find some of these activities to be suitable for homework assignments.

EXTENDING THE BOOK

1. Make a Big Book. Use the Important Dates page at the back of *A Picture Book of George Washington* to help you plan with the students what they would like to record about Washington's life. Assign groups to complete each page.

2. Learn about the first flag, using the worksheet on page 42. (Note: The often-seen circular star formation is not supported by historical evidence.) Extend with this activity: Count the number of stars and stripes on our present U.S. flag. Compare the first and the present flag in a Venn diagram. Learn about flag etiquette and how to take care of a flag properly. Discuss the words to the Pledge of Allegiance. (Both flag etiquette and the Pledge of Allegiance appear on page 43.) Students can create their own artistic flags with gummed stars, and white, red, and blue paper.

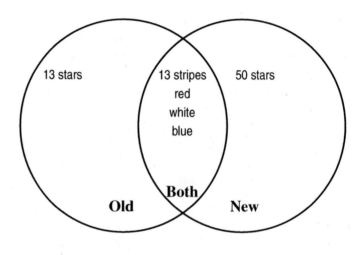

3. Research Francis Scott Key. Listen to and learn the national anthem. You may wish to read *The Star-Spangled Banner,* illustrated by Peter Spier. Words to "The Star Spangled Banner" can be found on page 64. Make a class star-spangled banner. Spread a length of white butcher paper on the floor. Direct the students to draw a thin line of liquid white glue. Sprinkle with red or blue glitter. When dry, shake off the excess glitter. Add gummed paper stars to the picture. Hang the banner on the wall.

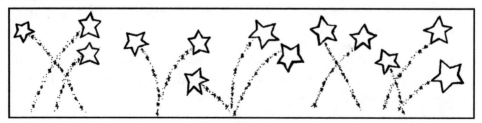

4. Make a little book about ways we remember the three great American leaders studied here. Reproduce pages 55–57. Have students make a cover and add any pages they wish. Staple and send home to share.

Picture This!

Read each sentence below. Choose one. Cut it out and glue it onto a piece of paper. Draw a picture to illustrate the sentence.

Young George liked to fish and go boating.

Washington's best subject was arithmetic.

George liked to survey fields and forests.

At 16, George was very tall.

Washington was a good leader against the French.

George Washington became known as a brave man.

George married a wealthy widow.

The English won the long war with France.

Extension: Have students use all of the sentences to create their own books about George Washington.

Creative Writing Projects

All of the creative writing projects below tie in nicely with the text of *A Picture Book of George Washington*. Choose those activities which best suit the needs and abilities of your students. Projects may be assigned as individual, partner, or group assignments. Some may be appropriate homework activities.

- Young George liked to fish and go boating. Most of all, he liked to ride his horse. Draw a picture and write a story about your favorite hobby.

- George learned to read and write in school. He practiced his handwriting by copying lists of classroom rules. Copy a list of your classroom rules or write a list of your own rules. Use your best handwriting.

- George's favorite school subject was arithmetic. What is your favorite subject? Tell why you like that subject best.

- When George was eleven, his father died. He had to help his mother run the farm and watch his younger brothers and sisters. Tell how you help out at your home.

- King George III of England wanted to tax the colonies, but they refused to pay. Write a story and draw a picture of what the colonists in Boston did with tea to protest the taxes.

- George Washington was chosen to lead the colonies' fight against England. Often there were not enough uniforms, food, or blankets for his soldiers. Tell how you would feel if you were a soldier then and it was cold and snowing.

- Explain why you think George Washington is called the "Father of Our Country."

- Write some ways in which you are like George Washington, or write some ways in which you are different than George Washington. Make a chart to show these likenesses and differences.

- Write about Presidents' Day and what it means.

- Use the story frame on page 45 to write a story about Washington. Share your story with someone at home.

A Picture Book of George Washington

Number Words Puzzle

Read each fact about George Washington.
Fill in the blank with the correct number name.
Use the Word Bank to help you.
Write the number name in the crossword puzzle.

Word Bank

twenty-one	eight	thirteen
sixty-seven	twenty-six	eleven

Across

2. George married Martha when he was _ _ _ _ _ _ - _ _ **x**

4. George was president for _ _ **g** _ _ years.

5. His father died when George was _ _ _ **v** _ _ .

Down

1. George was _ _ _ _ _ _ - _ _ _ _ **n** years old when he died.

2. The _ _ _ **r** _ _ _ _ colonies became states.

3. George joined the Virginia army when he was _ _ _ _ _ _ _ - **o** _ _

* On the back of this paper write the events in correct story order.

A "Washington" Map

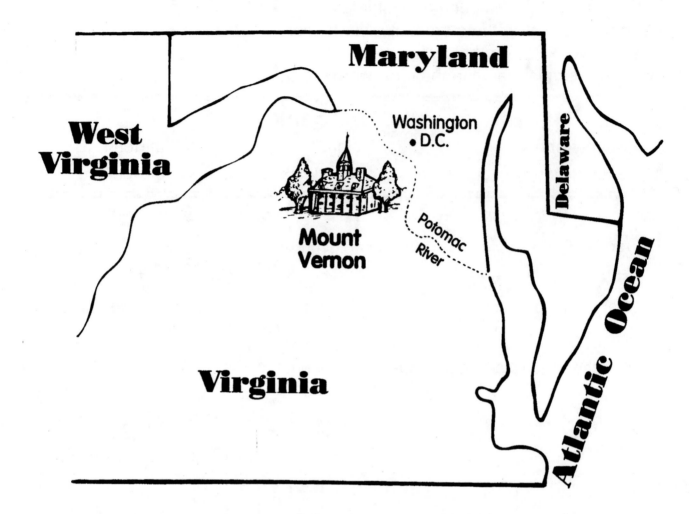

Follow the directions below. All answers can be found on the map above.

1. Find Washington, D.C. On the (•) draw a (✪) and color it yellow.

2. Draw a purple line south from Washington, D.C. to Mount Vernon.

3. Color Mount Vernon orange.

4. In which state is Mount Vernon? _____ Color this state green.

5. Find the Atlantic Ocean. Color it blue.

6. Write the name of the river that is next to Washington, D.C.

   _____.

Fun with Math

Here are some fun math activities to incorporate into your thematic unit. Each of the assignments below is related to the text of *A Picture Book of George Washington*.

*One-to-One Correspondence

After the war between the colonies and England ended, the 13 colonies became 13 states. Direct the students to draw 13 squares—one for each colony. Then tell them to draw 13 stars—one for each state. Draw a line from each colony to each state. Follow up with page 42.

*Sets

The war between England and the colonies lasted eight years. George was eleven years old when his father died. At sixteen, George was very tall. Present one of these facts (or any other of your choosing) to the students. Give each child a paper plate and some markers (dried beans, cereal, buttons, etc.). Tell them to make a set on the plate to represent the number in the sentence. Read another sentence and follow the same procedure.

*Measuring and Estimating

George used his father's surveying tools to measure a turnip field and a small pine forest. Let students measure their heights, waists, wrists, or ankles using this method. Give students rolls of string or yarn and scissors. Direct them to cut off the amount of string they think will just fit around their wrist or to cut a piece they estimate to be the same length as their height. (You may want to have partners work together for this project.) Then have them compare their estimates with strings cut to actual lengths. Afterwards, discuss how well they were able to estimate.

*Number Names

Pair students for this activity. Direct them to find examples of number names in the text. "In 1753, when George Washington was twenty-one. . . ." Have them write the number name and its corresponding numeral. Follow up with page 37.

*Calendars

In April, 1775, fighting broke out between England and the colonies. One month later, leaders of the thirteen colonies met in Philadelphia. Have students identify the next month. Ask what month it is now and which month is next. Give each student a blank calendar. Have them fill in the dates for the coming month (see page 40).

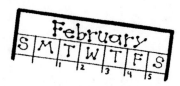

Blank Calendar

month

Sunday	Monday	Tuesday	Wednesday	Thursday	Friday	Saturday

This and That

Incorporate any of the following activities into your program wherever they are most effective and appropriate. Some ideas may be used as homework assignments.

- George Washington was a famous president. How many other presidents can you name? Who is our current president?

- The capital of the United States is named after Washington. How else is George Washington commemorated? (See page 58 for information on the Washington Monument. Examine coins and paper money; see page 48.)

- George liked to survey and make maps. Draw a map of your route to school or a map of your house.

- Virginia was one of the first colonies. Write the names of the thirteen colonies.

- Find the state of Virginia on a map. Locate Mount Vernon and Washington, D.C.

- Young George mapped a turnip field. Eat raw or cooked turnips. Draw and color a picture of a turnip.

- A story says that George chopped down a cherry tree. When his father asked him if he was responsible, he replied that he could not tell a lie. He had chopped down the cherry tree. George was being honest, but what if he had lied? Write a story about a lie he might have told or write a story about a lie that got you in trouble. (Extend this activity by reading some tall tales and having the students write their own tall tales. Stories about Paul Bunyan, John Henry, Slue-Foot Sue, and Pecos Bill would be appropriate and motivating.)

- Washington's Mount Vernon home was thirteen miles from the new capital. How far is just one mile? Go for a one mile walk or run one mile. Time yourself. How long would it take to go thirteen miles?

- In school, George wrote his math lessons with chalk, on a slate. Get your teacher's permission to practice your math on the chalkboard.

- George wrote with a quill and liquid ink. Find a fountain pen and write with it (may be available at stationery stores).

- Make rubbings of a quarter. Find Washington's picture on a $1 bill. Follow up with page 48.

Name _____

The First Flag

The first United States flag had thirteen stars and thirteen stripes. Trace the stars. Color the flag.

1 = red   2 = white   3 = blue

| 1 | 2 | 1 | 2 | 1 | 2 | 1 | 2 | 1 | 2 | 1 | 2 | 1 |

Honoring Our Flag

The United States flag is a symbol of our country. As good citizens, we should know how to honor our flag. Some important rules about caring for the U.S. flag are written below. Color each flag after you read the rule.

 Face the flag and place your right hand across your heart when you say the Pledge of Allegiance. The words to the Pledge of Allegiance are at the bottom of this page.

 When a U.S. flag passes by you in a parade, put your hand over your heart or give a military salute.

 Girls do not need to remove their hats when saluting a flag. Boys, however, must remove their hats.

 The flag should never be used to carry or hold anything, nor should it be used for clothing or a costume.

 Carefully fold and put away the flag when it is not in use.

 You may wash or mend a flag. If it is very damaged, you may destroy the flag by burning it.

 Usually the flag is displayed outside from sunrise to sunset. If it is flown at night, it should be spotlighted.

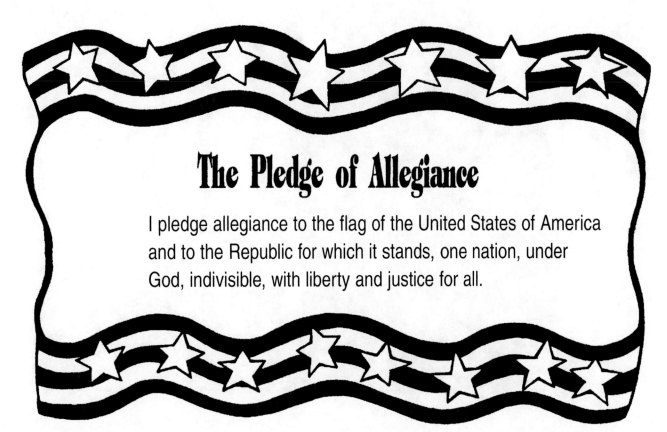

The Pledge of Allegiance

I pledge allegiance to the flag of the United States of America and to the Republic for which it stands, one nation, under God, indivisible, with liberty and justice for all.

Washington Word Bank

This Word Bank is a handy reference tool for creative writing, vocabulary development, social studies, and more. It can also be used with the story frame on page 45.

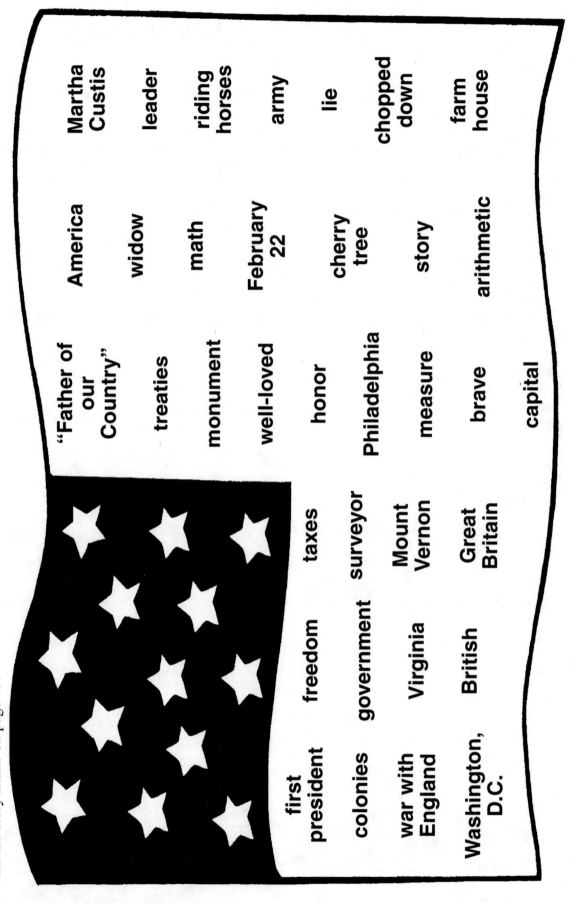

"Father of our Country"	America	Martha Custis
treaties	widow	leader
monument	math	riding horses
well-loved	February 22	army
honor	cherry tree	lie
Philadelphia	story	chopped down
measure	arithmetic	farm house
brave		
capital		

first president	freedom	taxes
colonies	government	surveyor
war with England	Virginia	Mount Vernon
Washington, D.C.	British	Great Britain

Story Frames

This writing strategy is great for beginning writers. An outline is provided for student use. Words to fill in the blanks can be chosen from prepared word banks (see pages 18, 31, and 44) or lists brainstormed by the class.

- Write a sample story frame on the chalkboard or overhead projector for everyone to see.

- Model with the students how to choose words from a word bank to fit into the frame.

- Direct the students to copy the story frame onto a sheet of paper or supply them with a prepared frame (see the sample below).

- Tell the students to fill in the blank spaces appropriately.

- Have them illustrate the text.

- Pair or group the students so they can share the stories with one another. Use this story frame to write about the famous men studied in this book.

Title

_____ was a great

_____. He was born in

_____. As a young boy he

liked to _____ and

_____. When he grew up he

became a _____.

Every year we honor him on a special day called

_____.

It is in the month of _____.

Name_____

Washington or Lincoln?

1. Read each word group below.

2. Color the 🪕 if the words tell about George Washington.

3. Color the 🏚 if the words tell about Abraham Lincoln.

4. Color the 🪕 and the 🏚 if the words tell about both George Washington and Abraham Lincoln.

a.  lived long ago

b. 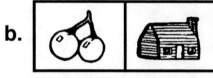 was a lawyer

c. 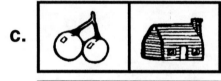 was a leader of the Army

d. 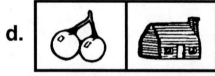 called the "Father of Our Country"

e. 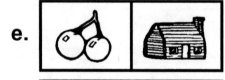 was born in a log cabin

f. 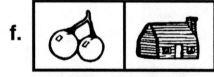 was a president

g.  walked miles to borrow books

h. 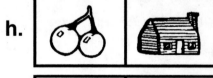 was honest

h. 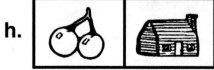 liked math

An Author's Life

Children may want to know something about the authors of the books they read. Some information about David A. Adler and Dee Lillegard is presented in the boxes below. Share some information with the students. You may want to try one of the suggested follow-up activities, which are designated by an asterisk (*), and based on other books by the authors.

David A. Adler

A Picture Book of Abraham Lincoln
and *A Picture Book of George Washington*

David A. Adler was born in New York City in 1947. His father was a teacher and his mother was a social worker. David attended college and graduated with a master's degree. As a professional artist, he has over 200 published drawings and cartoons in magazines and newspapers. He now teaches and writes full-time. Some of his diverse titles include *A Little at a Time* (Random House, 1976); *Roman Numerals* (Crowell, 1977); *Hanukkah Game Book* (Bonim Books, 1978); *Redwoods Are the Tallest Trees in the World* (Crowell, 1978).

- Find out about and learn how to write Roman numerals.

- Play some Hanukkah games.

Dee Lillegard

My First Martin Luther King Book

Dee Lillegard is a pseudonym for Deanna Quintel. This native Californian has worked as a children's book editor and now teaches writing for children in the San Francisco Bay area. Dee has written over 200 published stories, poems, and puzzles for children. In addition, she has written teacher support materials, including *September to September: Poems for All Year Round* (Childrens Press, 1986). Her other titles include *I Can Be a Plumber; I Can Be a Beautician; I Can Be an Electrician; I Can Be a Welder; My First Columbus Day Book* (all are published by Childrens Press).

- Have children tell or write about careers they would like to have.

- Dr. Seuss is a pseudonym. Find out his real name.

On the Money

Abraham Lincoln's face can be seen on a coin and a paper bill. George Washington's face also is on a coin and a bill.

    1. Cut and paste the correct face on each coin or bill.

    2. Color the penny copper and the quarter silver.

    3. Color the bills green.

Money Problems

Make enough copies of the page so that each child will get a task card. Cut apart the cards and place them in a paper lunch bag or empty shoebox. Let each child draw a card. Direct them to solve the problem. After all the students are ready, have them share their problems and solutions with the class. If you prefer, make a transparency of this page for use on an overhead projector. Assign a different problem daily. Have children make additional quarter and penny problems.

1
George has 4
Abe has 6
How many altogether?

5
Abe has 10
He spent 3
How many left?

2
Martin has 1
How many is that?

6
George has 2
Martin has 1
Who has more money?

3
Abe has 8
Martin has 2
How many coins?
How much money altogether?

7
George has 5
Martin has 5
How many coins?
How much money altogether?

4
George has 10
He spent 4
How many left?
How much money is left?

8
Abe has two
How many is that?

Star Pencil Poke

Directions

- Copy the star pattern onto white or colored card stock.
- Cut out the star shape and punch holes at points.
- Write a different math problem next to each hole punched.
- Turn over the star shape; write answers next to the corresponding holes.
- If desired, laminate the star, cut out, and re-punch the holes.
- Staple two craft sticks together to the bottom of the star, placing one stick on each side of it.

To Play

- One child faces the front of the star while another child faces the back.
- The child facing the front places a pencil, straw, or golf tee through a hole and says the problem aloud. For example, in the left diagram below, if the child places the pencil in the far right hole he or she would say, "Seven plus one equals eight."
- The child facing the other side checks the answers.
- After all problems have been completed the children trade places.

Front

Back

Extensions

- Individual students can practice the problems on their own.
- Direct the children to write number sentences for all the problems on the stars.
- Do not label the star with problems before laminating. Use water-based pens to write problems. Change them as often as you need.

Flag Math

Use with page 42. Read the facts in the box. Write the number in the box. Solve.

Our First Flag Facts

- It has 13 stars.
- There are 13 stripes altogether.
- There are 7 red stripes.
- There are 6 white stripes.

1. The number of stars minus the number of white stripes

   ☐ 13 — ☐ 6 = ☐

2. The number of red stripes plus the number of stars

    — = ☐

3. The number of stars minus the number of stripes altogether

   ☐ — ☐ = ☐

4. The number of white stripes plus the number of red stripes

    — = ☐

5. The number of red stripes minus the number of white stripes

    — = ☐

* Draw the correct number of stars and stripes next to each problem.

Patriotic Flowers

Celebrate Presidents' Day with this colorful science experiment. Pair or group the children. Supply each pair or group with the list of materials below. Follow up the experiment with a Science Report (see page 53). Note: You may want to enlist older students or adult volunteers to help with this project.

Materials:

one white carnation; blue and red food coloring; two clear plastic cups; one knife; one plastic spoon or straw (for mixing); water; paper towels; newspaper

Procedure:

- Pour one inch of red food coloring into a cup.

- Add one inch (2.54 cm) of water to the food coloring.

- Mix with the spoon and set aside.

- Pour one inch (2.54 cm) of blue food coloring into the second cup.

- Add one inch (2.54 cm) of water to the food coloring.

- Wipe the spoon clean with a paper towel before mixing.

- Set the cup aside.

- Spread a thick layer of newspaper on a flat surface.

- With the knife, trim the flower until it is two inches taller than the cups.

- With the knife, carefully cut the stem in half along its length.

- Position the two cups of colored water side by side.

- Place one part of the stem into the red water and the other part of the stem into the blue water.

- Have the children predict what will happen. Record and save the responses for later use.

- Let the flower stand for a few hours.

- Compare the children's predictions with what actually happened.

- Discuss the process they observed.

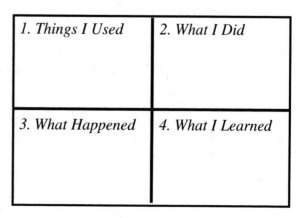

Extensions:

- Older children can write a Science Report after completing the experiment above. See page 53 for a prepared form.

- Younger children can write a picture report. Use page 54 or have them fold a 9" x 12" (or larger) sheet of construction paper in fourths. Label each segment as shown in the diagram at right. Direct the children to draw appropriate pictures in each segment. Encourage them to write words and/or sentences.

1. Things I Used	2. What I Did
3. What Happened	4. What I Learned

Science Report

Name _____ Date _____

Experiment: _____

Materials Used: _____

_____

_____

What I Did: _____

_____

_____

_____

_____

_____

_____

_____

_____

I Predicted: _____

_____

What Happened: _____

_____

_____

_____

What I Learned: _____

_____

_____

Experiment Report

Draw pictures to show your experiment.

1. Things I Used

2. What I Did

3. What Happened

2. What I Learned

Celebrate America
Little Book

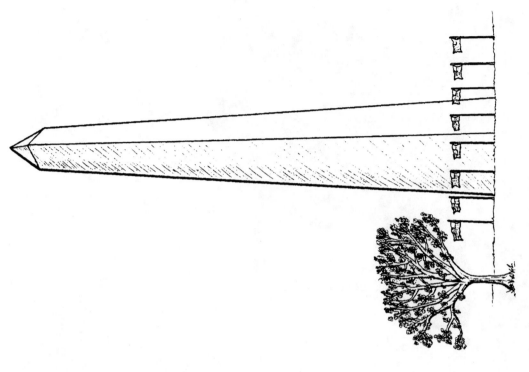

Washington Monument

In the middle of the National Mall is the Washington Monument. It was built to honor George Washington. It is as tall as a 46-story building. There are 897 steps to its top.

Capitol Building, Washington, D.C.

The capitol is the building where the lawmakers of the United States meet. It is in Washington, D.C. at one end of a long park called the National Mall. Washington, D.C. was named after our first president, George Washington.

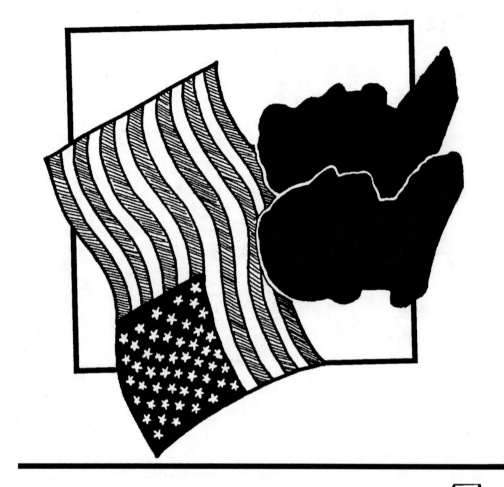

Presidents' Day

We remember our presidents on the third Monday in February, Presidents' Day. We especially remember Washington and Lincoln because their birthdays are in February.

Lincoln Memorial

At the other end of the Mall is the Lincoln Memorial. It helps us remember President Lincoln. It is a large building with a statue of Lincoln inside. The statue is almost as tall as a two-story building.

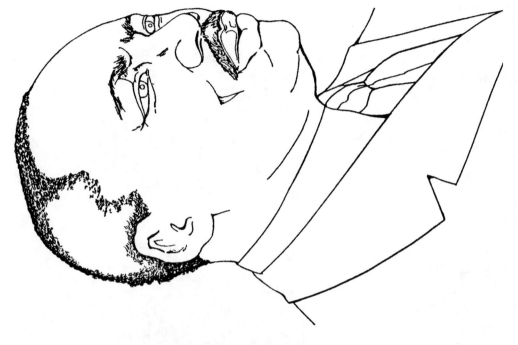

Martin Luther King, Jr. Day

In 1983, the Congress of the United States made the third Monday in January a federal holiday. On this day, we honor Martin Luther King, Jr. and remember his dream of freedom and equal rights for all people.

March on Washington

On August 28, 1963, over 250,000 people of all races came to Washington, D.C. They met on the Mall, in front of the Lincoln Memorial. Martin Luther King made his famous "I Have a Dream" speech that day.

Famous Buildings and Monuments

Read about the famous monuments below. Color each picture

The Thomas Jefferson Memorial was built in honor of our third President and author of the Declaration of Independence. A white marble dome tops this beautiful circular building. Inside is a 19-foot (5.8 meters) bronze statue of Jefferson.

The most famous house in America can be found at 1600 Pennsylvania Avenue in Washington, D.C. It is the White House, where the President of the United States lives and works. The White House is the oldest government building in Washington.

Mt. Vernon was the home of George Washington. It is about 13 miles south of the capital. Today, Mt. Vernon is a museum and you can tour the grounds. You will be able to see how people lived and worked in Washington's time.

Mt. Rushmore is a high cliff in the Black Hills of South Dakota. It was carved to resemble the faces of four American presidents. George Washington is at the left. Abraham Lincoln is on the far right. Each face is about as tall as a five-story building. (Thomas Jefferson is next to Washington; Theodore Roosevelt is next to Lincoln.)

A Three-Way Comparison

Read each word group. Color the box under the name of man the words describe. Sometimes there may be more than one answer.

	Washington	*Lincoln*	*Martin Luther King, Jr.*
1. born in February			
2. a great leader			
3. was shot			
4. liked to read			
5. was a minister			
6. was brave			
7. was a U.S. president			
8. led peace marches			
9. led an army			
10. born in January			

Teacher Note: Cover these directions before duplicating this page. If you prefer to review this page orally, draw three symbols or write the three names on the chalkboard. After reading a phrase, call on a student to go to the board and mark an **X** next to the correct answer(s).

Name_____

Which Is First?

Look at each pair of pictures. Color the one which came first.

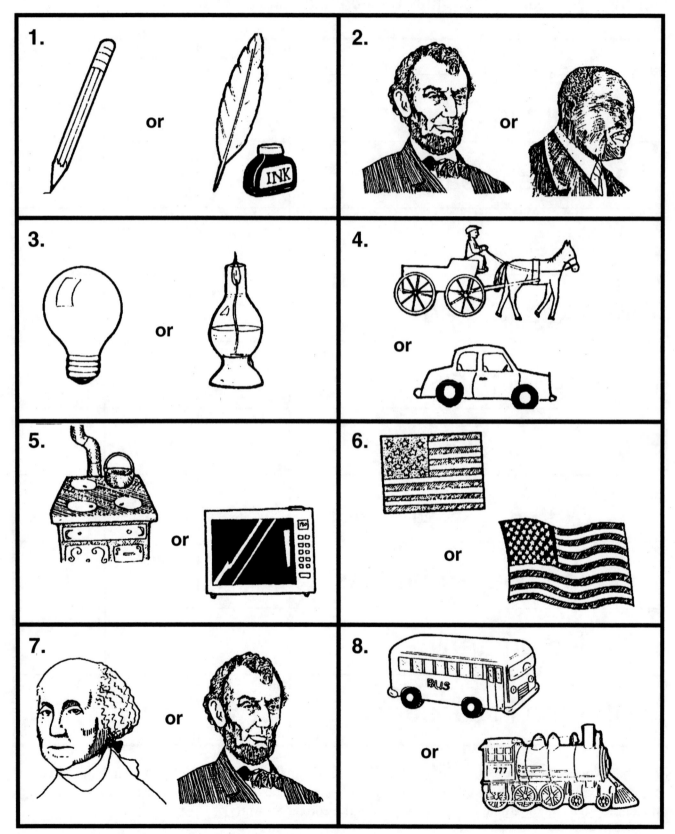

The Life and Times Of...

This teacher resource page is a compilation of facts about the times in which George Washington, Abraham Lincoln, and Martin Luther King, Jr. lived. Use them to help students get a historical perspective of these three men. Some ways to present these facts are outlined on page 62.

	George Washington	**Abraham Lincoln**	**Martin Luther King, Jr.**
Born Died	1732–1799	1809–1865	1929–1968
# of states	13	34 *(at beginning of his 1st term)*	50
Means of Transportation	Horseback Steamboats Sailing Ships Horse-drawn wagons and carriages	Railroads Flat boats Stagecoaches Covered wagons Horse-drawn streetcars	Automobiles Airplanes Buses Subways Motorcycles
Famous People	Thomas Jefferson, statesman John Adams, 1st vice-president Benjamin Franklin, inventor and statesman Daniel Boone, frontiersman	Edgar Allen Poe, author Elizabeth Blackwell, 1st woman doctor Hans Christian Anderson, writer Thomas Edison, inventor	The Beatles John F. Kennedy (died 1963) Rosa Parks Walt Disney (died 1966) Marilyn Monroe (died 1962)
Current Inventions	Franklin stove Bifocals Discovery of electricity Cotton gin	Oil lamps (1st one in 1857) Telegraph (1861) Sewing machine (1855) Chewing gum (1848)	Television Nuclear power Transistor radio Movie theaters Telephones Instant cameras Microwave ovens Computers
Popular Songs	"Yankee Doodle"	"Jingle Bells" (1856)	"Hey Jude" "Mrs. Robinson"
Historical Events	Boston Tea Party American Revolution Thanksgiving first celebrated as a national holiday in 1789	First baseball game (1846) First pencil with attached eraser (1858) Civil War began in 1861	Assassinations of John and Robert Kennedy and Martin Luther King-Beginning of Vietnam conflict-Alan B. Shepard was 1st American in space (1961)

Life and Times File Activities

The fact file on page 61 is intended for teacher use and reference. Listed below are some ways in which you can present the information to students.

1. Provide background information to the students through other books. To learn about Washington's time, read *Sam the Minuteman* or *George the Drummer Boy*, both by Nathaniel Benchley (Harper Row, 1969 and 1977 respectively). For some background on Lincoln, read excerpts from *True Stories About Abraham Lincoln* by Ruth B. Gross (Scholastic, 1973). Provide some historical perspective with passages from *Martin Luther King, Jr.: Free at Last* by David A. Adler (Holiday House, 1986). You may also use the excellent "If You..." series from Scholastic, which includes the titles *If You Grew Up with George Washington* by Ruth B. Gross (1985); *If You Grew Up with Abraham Lincoln* by Ann McGovern (1985); and *If You Lived at the Time of Martin Luther King* by Ellen Levine (1990).

2. Make time lines. Attach string or yarn to the chalkboard tray or across a corner of the room. Choose a specific topic, such as transportation. Establish the changes that took place over the years. On index cards, have the students draw pictures of some of these means of transportation. With clothespins, attach the cards to the line in chronological order. Another method to use: Make three columns on the chalkboard. Label them as shown in the diagram at left. On large self-stick notes, write the names of various vehicles. Have the students arrange the notes in the correct columns. Follow the same procedure to study famous people, inventions, or historical events.

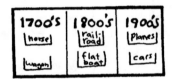

3. Use the information from the fact file to create Venn diagrams or charts. For example, compare the 1700s with the 1800s. A possible Venn diagram and a chart follow:

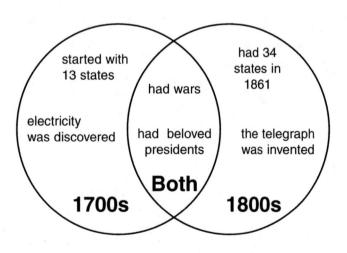

Famous People	
1700s	1800s
Benjamin Franklin	Thomas Edison
Daniel Boone	Elizabeth Blackwell
John Adams	Edgar Allen Poe

4. Expand the fact file with other categories. Learn what clothes were in style, what games children played, what forms of entertainment were available, etc.

Presidential Projects

These two art projects are both appropriate and fun ways to celebrate Presidents' Day. Be sure to buy extra pretzels when you make log cabins. Students may find the snack food hard to resist.

Log Cabins

Materials: one-half pint milk containers (cleaned and dried); stick pretzels; white household glue; plastic knives; wax paper

Directions:

- Line a flat surface with wax paper.
- With the knife, cut the pretzels to fit the sides and top of the carton.
- Spread one line of glue at a time on the carton.
- Apply the cut pretzels to the glue; press in place.
- Continue in this manner until all sides and the top are covered.
- **Variation:** If the project above is too difficult for your students, try this idea instead. With a brown crayon, draw a log cabin outline on a sheet of drawing paper. Glue lengths of stick pretzels to the log cabin.

Marbleized Paper

Materials: red and blue food coloring; cooking oil; water; empty, clean margarine cups; cake pan; stirrers (spoons, craft sticks, etc.); finger painting paper; newspaper

Directions:

- In the margarine cup, mix red food coloring with a few drops of oil; set aside (1).
- In another cup, mix blue food coloring with a few drops of oil, set aside.
- Fill the cake pan with one-half inch (1.25 cm) of water (2).
- Pour circles of red food coloring/oil mix over the surface of the water.
- Pour circles of blue food coloring/oil mix over the water's surface (3).
- Carefully lay a sheet of finger painting paper on the water's surface (4).
- Lift up and place on newspaper to dry.

Freedom Songs

To help students learn the words to the songs on this page, enlist the aid of parents, other adults, or siblings. Send this sheet home with students. Include a note to parents asking them to review the words with their children. You may want to focus on one song at a time, so write dates beside each to designate when they should be studied.

The Star Spangled Banner

Oh, say, can you see, by the dawn's early light, What so proudly we hailed at the twilight's last gleaming, Whose broad stripes and bright stars, through the perilous fight, O'er the ramparts we watched were so gallantly streaming? And the rocket's red glare, the bombs bursting in air, Gave proof through the night that our flag was still there Oh, say, does that Star Spangled Banner yet wave, O'er the land of the free and the home of the brave?

We Shall Overcome

We shall overcome
We shall overcome
We shall overcome some day.

Chorus:

Oh, deep in my heart
I do believe
We shall overcome some day.

2. We'll walk hand in hand,

Chorus

3. The truth will make us free,

Chorus

4. We shall live in peace,

Chorus

America the Beautiful

O beautiful for spacious skies,
For amber waves of grain,
For purple mountain majesties
Above the fruited plain!
America! America!
God shed his grace on thee,
And crown thy good with brotherhood
From sea to shining sea!

America

My country, tis of thee,
Sweet land of liberty,
Of thee I sing.
Land where my fathers died,
Land of the Pilgrims' pride.
From ev'ry mountainside
Let freedom ring.

Patriotic Desserts

Students will enjoy preparing these refreshing desserts. Not only are they tasty, they are quick and easy to make.

Red, White, and Blue Parfaits

Ingredients

cherry gelatin

blueberry gelatin

whipped cream

- Prepare the cherry and blueberry gelatins (keep separate).
- After the gelatin has set, spoon a layer of the blueberry gelatin into a clear plastic cup or glass.
- Add a layer of whipped cream.
- Top with a layer of cherry gelatin.
- Enjoy!

Cool Berries

- Cut up the strawberries if desired.
- Place a layer of blueberries into an ice cream dish or clear plastic cup.
- Scoop some ice cream over the blueberries.
- Top the ice cream with strawberries.
- **Variation:** Mash some blueberries and mix with vanilla ice cream. Set aside. Repeat with raspberries or strawberries. Layer with the blueberry mix on the bottom, plain ice cream in the middle, and the raspberry or strawberry mix on top.

Ingredients

raspberries or strawberries

blueberries

vanilla ice cream or vanilla yogurt

Cool Salad

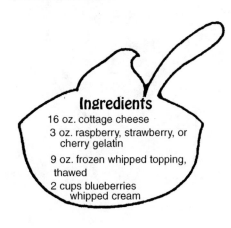

Ingredients

16 oz. cottage cheese

3 oz. raspberry, strawberry, or cherry gelatin

9 oz. frozen whipped topping, thawed

2 cups blueberries
whipped cream

- In a large bowl, mix the cottage cheese and the gelatin.
- Fold in the frozen whipped topping, thawed.
- Spoon the mixture into individual serving cups.
- Top with a dollop of whipped cream.
- Sprinkle with some blueberries.

1-2-3 Dessert

1. Fill a bowl with fresh strawberries and blueberries.
2. Pour some cream into the bowl.
3. Eat with a spoon.

Patriotic Picnic

Host an indoor picnic to honor Washington, Lincoln, and King. If possible, use the school multipurpose room or other large area. Sample decorations, activities, and refreshments are described below. Choose those ideas which are best-suited for your teaching style and students' skill levels and interests.

Decorating

- Make tablecloths from red, white, and blue butcher paper. Tape the edges to the table.

- Fill red, white, and blue balloons with helium (helium tanks may be available for rental through your local card and party shop). Attach a string to each one. Gather them closely and tie them together. Attach red, white, and blue crepe paper streamers to the gathered section of the balloons. Drape the streamers loosely around the table; tape them to the table (see diagram).

- Weave red, white, and blue construction paper place mats or laminate glitter and star-decorated paper place mats (see page 67 for both ideas).

Activities

- Sing or listen to patriotic songs. (See pages 64 and 67 for some suggested titles and sources.)

- Conduct interviews. Divide the class into three groups. Choose one person in the first group to represent Washington, one person from the second group to represent Lincoln, and one person from the third group to represent Martin Luther King. Have the others in each group ask their representative a question such as, "George, what was your favorite subject in school?" George might answer that he enjoyed math most. Rehearse the interviews before having each group present their skit to the rest of the class.

- Play George Washington Scramble, Flag Toss, or Dr. King Says. Directions and rules for all three games can be found on page 68.

- Learn some traditional dances. (See page 68 for suggestions.)

Refreshments

- Some easy recipes to try are on page 65.

- Red fruit punch is a perfect drink.

Patriotic Picnic *(cont.)*

This page contains the how-to's for the decorations and activities on page 66.

Woven Place Mats

- Each child will need one sheet of white construction paper and red and blue construction paper strips (strips should be cut about one inch/ 2.54 cm wide).

- Fold the sheet of construction paper in half and cut lines to within one inch of the fold. (You may want to draw inch-wide/2.54 cm lines on the paper to act as guidelines for the students.)

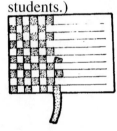

- Open up the folded sheet. Demonstrate how to weave the strips over and under through the slits. Space may be left between the strips or they may be moved tightly against one another. When the project is complete, laminate with clear self-stick paper or use a laminator (this last step is optional).

Star Decorated Place Mats

- Each child will need a sheet of white construction paper. You will also need to supply: white household glue; red and blue glitter; gummed paper stars.

- Have the students draw a thick squiggly line of glue on the construction paper. Immediately pour glitter on the glue line.

- Tell them to make some more glitter lines in the same manner.

- Let dry. Gently shake off the excess glitter onto newspaper or into a wastebasket.

- Glue stars onto the surface. Laminate with clear self-stick paper or a laminating machine.

Freedom Songs

- See page 64 for the words to some favorite tunes.

- Listen to some American favorites. *Wee Sing America: Songs of Patriots and Pioneers* (Pamela Conn Beal and Susan Hagen Nipp; Price Stern Sloan) is available on cassette tape.

- The cassette album, *Holly Daze,* by Mary Miche (from Song Trek, 2600 Hillegass, Berkeley, CA 94704) includes "The Dream of Martin Luther King."

- The sheet music to "We Shall Overcome" can be found in the book *If You Lived at the Time of Martin Luther King* by Ellen Levine (Scholastic, 1990) or *Martin Luther King: The Peaceful Warrior* by Ed Clayton (Simon & Schuster, 1968).

Patriotic Picnic *(cont.)*

George Washington Scramble

- Divide the class into small groups of three or four.

- Prepare one set of cards from page 69 for each group. Copy onto index stock or construction paper for extra stability. Cut apart a page of letters and place them into a paper lunch bag. Make one bag of letters for each group.

- Distribute the paper bags.

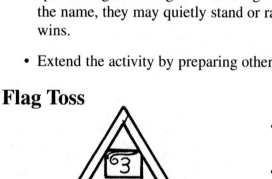

- On a given signal, the groups are to assemble the letters to spell George Washington. When a group has completed the name, they may quietly stand or raise their hands. The first group to correctly spell the name wins.

- Extend the activity by preparing other cards with different names.

Flag Toss

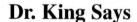

- With masking tape, make a two-foot (.6m) triangle on a tabletop or uncarpeted floor.

- Copy page 70 and cut out the flags. Tape them inside the triangular border as shown.

- Make a masking tape line about 12" (.3m) from the triangular base line. Have the students stand behind this line as they toss coins (or bean bags).

- Each player gets five coins to toss onto the flags. A coin must be inside the flag for it to count.

- Add up each player's numbers. The person with the highest score wins.

Dr. King Says

- This is a variation on Simon Says.

- Model some commands for the students: "Dr. King says march for peace." Other words to substitute for march include clap your hands, snap your fingers, shake your head, raise your hand, turn around, jump, run in place, etc.

- See what other commands your students can devise.

Dances

- Some dances to learn include the Virginia reel, which was popular in early America, and the waltz. Enlist the physical education teacher to teach these dances to the students.

- In the early '60s, the twist was very popular. Listen to music by Chubby Checker and do the twist.

George Washington Scramble

See page 68 for directions on using this page.

R	A	N	N
O	W	I	O
E	E	H	T
G	G	S	G

Flag Toss

See page 68 for directions on using this page.

Three Great Leaders
Bulletin Board

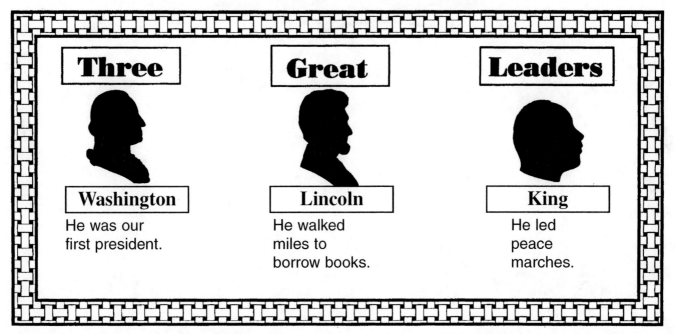

Objective: To establish, review, and compare information about George Washington, Abraham Lincoln, and Martin Luther King, Jr.

Materials: Red and blue butcher paper; red, white, and blue crepe paper; black and white construction paper; stapler or push pins; scissors

Construction:

- Line the bulletin board with red butcher paper.
- Reproduce the bulletin board title—Three Great Leaders (pages 75 and 76) onto white construction paper.
- Cut out and attach to the bulletin board background with staples.
- Reproduce the three silhouettes (pages 72 to 74) onto regular copy paper.
- Place each silhouette on a sheet of black construction paper.
- Attach the black silhouettes to the background with staples or push pins.
- Reproduce the labels (pages 76 and 77) onto white construction paper.
- Cut out and attach below the corresponding silhouettes.
- Cut three sheets of blue butcher paper to fit below each silhouette.
- Attach to the background with staples or push pins.
- To create a border twist the red, white, and blue crepe paper together.
- Line the bulletin board perimeter with the multi-colored twists.

Uses:

- Write information about the men in the appropriate sections.
- Draw comparisons about the three leaders using the information gathered.

Three Great Leaders
Bulletin Board *(cont.)*

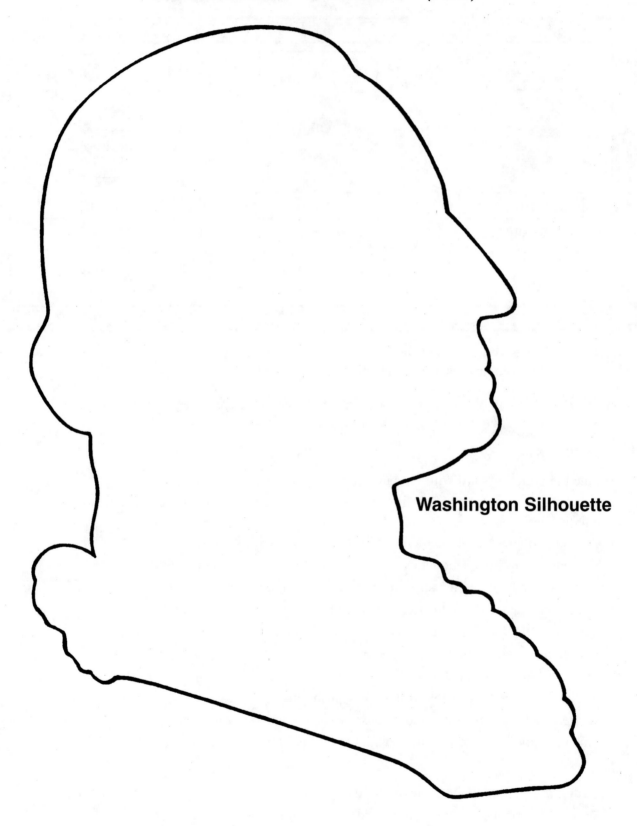

Washington Silhouette

Three Great Leaders
Bulletin Board *(cont.)*

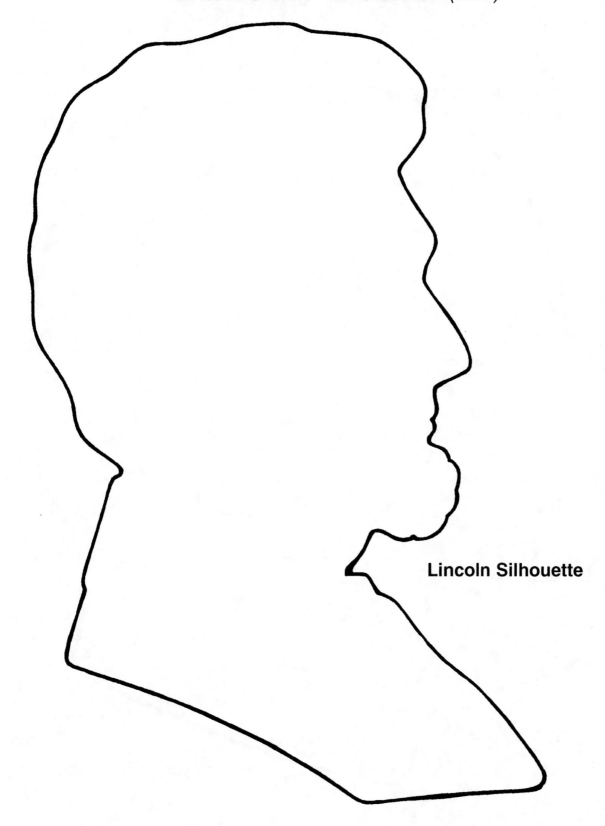

Lincoln Silhouette

Three Great Leaders
Bulletin Board *(cont.)*

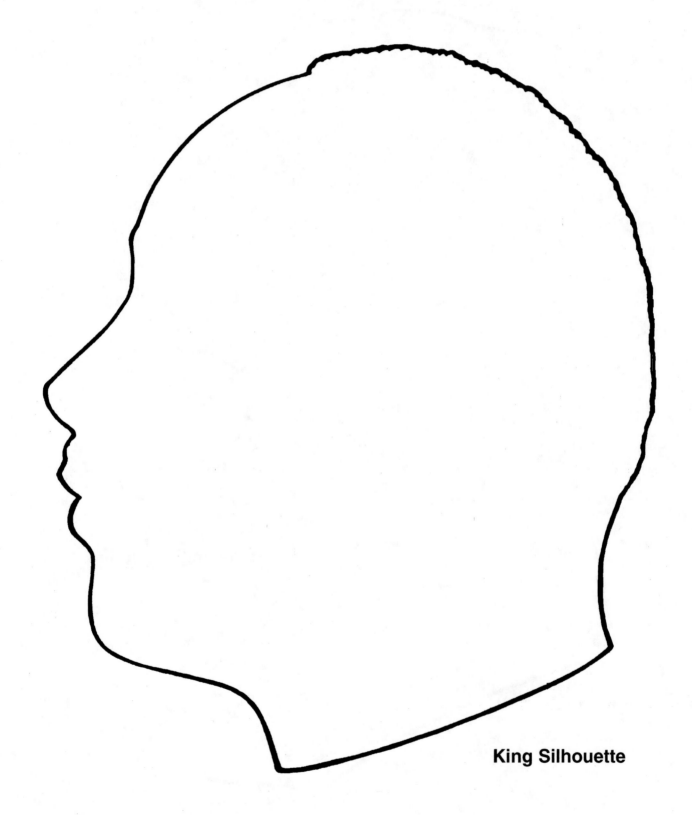

King Silhouette

Three Great Leaders
Bulletin Board *(cont.)*

Three Great Leaders
Bulletin Board *(cont.)*

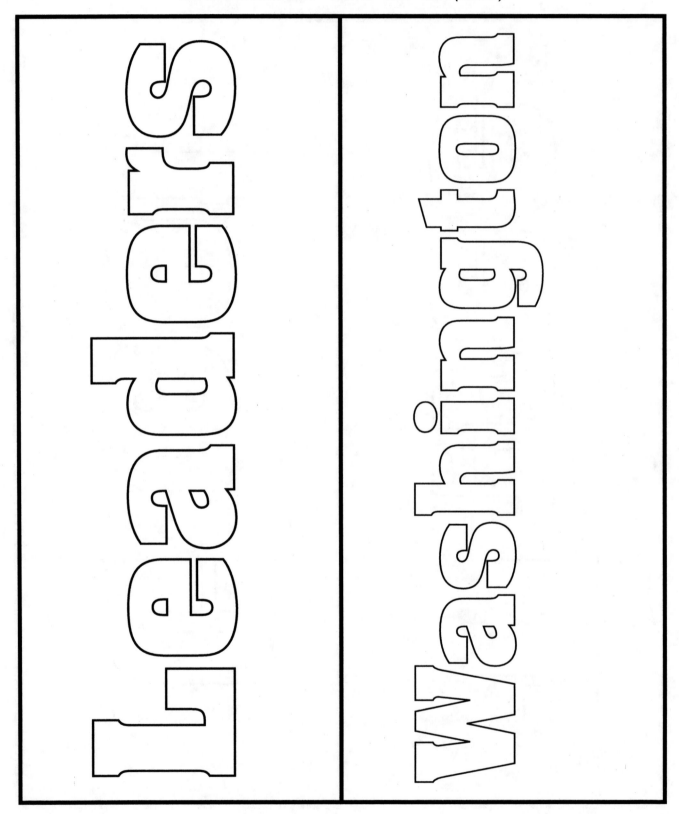

Three Great Leaders
Bulletin Board *(cont.)*

Stationery

Choose a border from those on this page to duplicate at the top of plain or lined paper for notes home, invitations, awards, homework reminders, or creative writing assignments.

Answer Key

Page 14

2. p e a c e f u l
1.   c h u r c h
6.   e q u a l
7.   N o b e l
5.   d r e a m
3.   p a s t o r
4.   m a r c h e s

Page 16

March on Washington

Page 26

1. 39 cents
2. 63 cents
3. 67 cents
4. 83 cents
5. 39 cents
6. 91 cents

Page 27

1. secret messages
2. Answers will vary.
3. Answers will vary.

Page 28

Answers will be according to the year and your state

Page 30

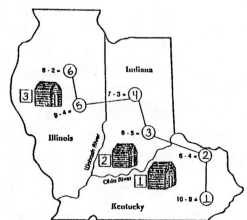

Page 46

a. both
b. Log cabin
c. cherries
d. cherries
e. log cabin
f. both
g. log cabin
h. both
i. cherries

Page 48

$5.00—Lincoln
$1.00—Washington
quarter—Washington
penny—Lincoln

Page 49

1. 10 pennies
2. 25 pennies
3. 10, 58 cents
4. 6 pennies, 6 cents
5. 7 pennies
6. George
7. 10 quarters, $2.50
8. 50 pennies

Page 51

1. 13 - 6 = 7
2. 7 + 13 = 20
3. 13 - 13 = 0
4. 6 + 7 = 13
5. 7 - 6 = 1

Page 59

1. W, L
2. all 3
3. L, K
4. all 3
5. K
6. all 3
7. W, L
8. K
9. W
10. K

Bibliography

Literature

Adler, David A. *A Picture Book of Abraham Lincoln.* Holiday House, 1989.

   A Picture Book of George Washington. Holiday House, 1989.

   A Picture Book of Martin Luther King, Jr. Scholastic, 1989.

Boone-Jones, Margaret. *Martin Luther King, Jr. A Picture Story.* Childrens Press, 1968.

Cary, Barbara. *Meet Abraham Lincoln.* Random House, 1989.

Crenson, Victoria. *Abraham Lincoln. An Adventure in Courage.* Troll, 1992.

   Martin Luther King, Jr. An Adventure in Courage. Troll, 1992.

   George Washington. An Adventure in Courage. Troll, 1992.

d'Aulaire, Ingri and Edgar Parin. *Abraham Lincoln.* Doubleday, 1939 and 1957.

   George Washington, Doubleday, 1936.

Fritz, Jean. *George Washington's Breakfast.* Coward McCann, Inc., 1974.

Green, Carol. *Abraham Lincoln. President of a Country Divided.* Childrens Press, 1991.

Gross, Ruth Belov. *True Stories About Abraham Lincoln.* Scholastic, 1973.

Lillegard, Dee. *My First Martin Luther King Book.* Childrens Press, 1987.

Livingston, Myra Cohn. *Let Freedom Ring: A Ballad of Martin Luther King, Jr.* Holiday House, 1992.

Lowery, Linda. *Martin Luther King Day.* Lerner, 1987.

Provense, Alice. *The Buck Stops Here.* Harper & Row, 1990.

Roop, Peter and Corinne. *Buttons for General Washington.* Carolrhoda Books, 1986.

Santrey, Laurence. *George Washington, Young Leader.* Troll, 1982.

Spier, Peter (illus. by). *The Star-Spangled Banner.* Doubleday, 1973.

Waber, Bernard. *Just Like Abraham Lincoln.* Scholastic, 1964.

Reference

Beal, Pamela Conn and Susan Hagen Nipp. *Wee Sing America. Songs of Patriots and Pioneers.* Price Stern Sloan, 1987.

Clark, Diane C. *A Kid's Guide to Washington, D.C.* Harcourt Brace Janovich, 1989.

Corwin, Judith Hoffman. *Patriotic Fun.* Julian Messner, 1985.

Freedman, Russell. *Lincoln: A Photobiography.* Clarion Books, 1987.

Goodman, Beth. *A Picture Book of the U.S. A.* Scholastic, 1991.

Gross, Ruth Belov. *If You Grew Up with George Washington.* Scholastic, 1982.

Levine, Elleny. *If You Lived at the Time of Martin Luther King.* Scholastic, 1990.

McGovern, Ann. *If You Grew Up with Abraham Lincoln.* Scholastic, 1966.

Prelutsky, Jack, selected by. *Random House Book of Poetry for Children.* Random House, 1983.